World Black History

the Building Future

Elizabeth Cregan

www.heinemannlibrary.co.uk
Visit our website to find out more information about Heinemann Library books.

To order:

☎ Phone +44 (0) 1865 888066

▤ Fax +44 (0) 1865 314091

▣ Visit www.heinemannlibrary.co.uk

Heinemann Library is an imprint of Capstone Global Library Limited, a company incorporated in England and Wales having its registered office at 7 Pilgrim Street, London, EC4V 6LB – Registered company number: 6695582

"Heinemann" is a registered trademark of Pearson Education Limited, under licence to Capstone Global Library Limited

Text © Capstone Global Library Limited 2010
First published in hardback in 2010
The moral rights of the proprietor have been asserted.

Edited by David Andrews, Abby Colich, and Louise Galpine
Designed by Ryan Frieson and Betsy Wernert
Illustrated by Mapping Specialists
Picture research by Mica Brancic
Originated by Heinemann Library
Printed in China by China Translation and Printing Services, Ltd.

ISBN 978 0 431194 06 6 (hardback)
14 13 12 11 10
10 9 8 7 6 5 4 3 2 1

British Library Cataloguing in Publication Data
Cregan, Elizabeth R.
Building the future. – (World black history)
909'.0496-dc22
A full catalogue record for this book is available from the British Library

Acknowledgements

We would like to thank the following for permission to reproduce photographs: ©Alamy p. **6** (tompiodesign.com); ©Corbis pp. **10** (Corbis Saba/Louise Gubb), **18** (Hulton-Deutsch Collection), **21** (Zen Icknow), **25** (Steve Starr), **26** (Bettman), **27** (Peter Turnley), **30** (Kurt Krieger), **31** (Jeff Albertson), **33** (ZUMA/Lonny Shavelson), **34** (Sygma/Patrick Robert), **35** (Sygma/Sophie Elbaz), **37** (Louise Gubb), **38** (Reuters/Ralph Orlowski), **40** (Dallas Morning News/Richard Michael Pruitt); ©Empics p. **32** (PA Photos); ©Getty Images pp. **4** (John Goodwin), **7** (AFP Photo/Desmond Kwande), **8** (AFP/Alexander Joe), **9** (Nelson Mandela Foundation/Juda Ngwenya), **11** (AFP PHOTO/Timothy A. Clary), **13** (David Fenton), **14** (Liaison/John Chiasson), **15** (Time Life Pictures/Image Works/Image Works/James Nubile), **17** (AFP Photo/Paul J. Richards), **19** (Hulton Archive/Keystone/Simon Dack/David Levenson), **20** (Jeremy O'Donnell), **23** (AFP Photo/Roberto Schmidt), **24** (Keystone), **29** (Ethan Miller), **36** (Tom Stoddart), **42** (Dave Hogan), **43** (Per-Anders Pettersson); ©iStock p. **22** (Peeter Viisimaa); ©Lonely Planet Images p. **39** (Tom Cockrem); ©PA Photos p. **41** (Landov/MCT/Chuck Kennedy).

Cover photograph of Democratic presidential hopeful Senator Barack Obama speaking to supporters at Truman Memorial Building in Missouri, USA, on 30 June 2008, reproduced with permission from Corbis/epa/Image by © Larry W. Smith.

We would like to thank Stephanie Davenport and Marika Sherwood for their invaluable help in the preparation of this book.

Every effort has been made to contact copyright holders of any material reproduced in this book. Any omissions will be rectified in subsequent printings if notice is given to the publisher.

Disclaimer
All the Internet addresses (URLs) given in this book were valid at the time of going to press. However, due to the dynamic nature of the Internet, some addresses may have changed, or sites may have changed or ceased to exist since publication. While the author and Publishers regret any inconvenience this may cause readers, no responsibility for any such changes can be accepted by either the author or the Publishers.

Contents

Some words are shown in bold, **like this**. You can find out what they mean by looking in the Glossary.

Closer to equality

By 1968 black Britons were legally protected from **discrimination**. They could not be denied job promotions, education, or housing because of their race. Many had left the inner cities for safer suburban areas, found skilled jobs, and entered the middle class.

Under the leadership of Martin Luther King, the Civil Rights Movement in the United States had also made progress. New laws protected African Americans from racial discrimination. Many held skilled jobs and earned enough money to live in better homes and send their children to university.

However, life did not improve for all black people. The new laws did not lead to true equality. Many still held low-paying jobs and lived in poor inner-city neighbourhoods. There was racial tension in many British cities, and in the US cities of Newark and Detroit frustration at continuing inequality had resulted in rioting. Reflecting on the cause of the riots, a government report concluded that "Our nation is moving toward two societies, one black, one white – separate and unequal."

Martin Luther King helped African Americans move closer to equality.

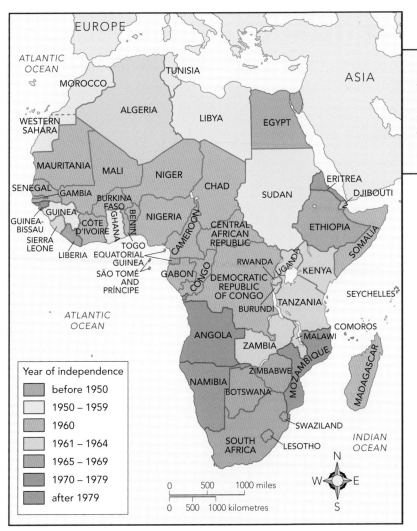

EUROPE

ATLANTIC OCEAN

ASIA

By 1993 all African nations were independent of European rule. This map shows the years each nation won its independence.

TUNISIA
MOROCCO
ALGERIA
LIBYA
EGYPT
WESTERN SAHARA
MAURITANIA
MALI
NIGER
SENEGAL
GAMBIA
BURKINA FASO
CHAD
SUDAN
ERITREA
DJIBOUTI
GUINEA
GHANA
BENIN
NIGERIA
GUINEA-BISSAU
CÔTE D'IVOIRE
SIERRA LEONE
LIBERIA
TOGO
EQUATORIAL GUINEA
CAMEROON
CENTRAL AFRICAN REPUBLIC
ETHIOPIA
SOMALIA
SÃO TOMÉ AND PRÍNCIPE
GABON
CONGO
DEMOCRATIC REPUBLIC OF CONGO
RWANDA
UGANDA
KENYA
BURUNDI
TANZANIA
SEYCHELLES

ATLANTIC OCEAN

COMOROS
ANGOLA
ZAMBIA
MALAWI
MOZAMBIQUE
MADAGASCAR
ZIMBABWE
NAMIBIA
BOTSWANA
SWAZILAND
SOUTH AFRICA
LESOTHO

INDIAN OCEAN

Year of independence
- before 1950
- 1950 – 1959
- 1960
- 1961 – 1964
- 1965 – 1969
- 1970 – 1979
- after 1979

0   500   1000 miles
0   500   1000 kilometres

N
W   E
S

Africa and the Caribbean

There were 40 independent African nations by 1968. Many struggled to build **democracies**. **Colonial** rulers had run most aspects of society for years. Few people native to these countries had the experience needed to run an independent nation. These nations were home to hundreds of different **ethnic** groups. This made it difficult to win popular support and create fair and free societies.

After centuries of slavery and colonial rule, many blacks in the Caribbean lived in poverty. Since Britain and the United States restricted immigration from this region, most blacks were unable to leave. In Brazil blacks worked to gain equal rights, but progress was very slow.

Creating a new Africa

The newly independent African nations faced many challenges. For years **colonial** rulers had run most of their businesses, banks, and shipping.

The Europeans had decided the boundaries of the African countries they created. They ignored old borders and the hundreds of different **ethnic** groups living within the new borders. With different languages, customs, and ways of life thrown together, the peoples within these new borders did not always want to live under the same political leadership.

Before independence some Africans were educated in Europe and the United States. But when they returned home, few top government jobs were available to them. Few African leaders could gain high-level experience. Many became involved in campaigns for greater freedoms and equality.

The African Union

In 1963 more than 30 African nations joined to form the Organization of African Unity (OAU). It was renamed the African Union (AU) in 2002. The AU fights illnesses, such as **malaria** and **AIDS**. It campaigns for fair trade and helps keep peace across Africa.

This is the flag of the African Union.

Independent nations struggle

After achieving independence, the new leaders faced many challenges. They had to learn to run their own businesses and banks. They also had to find the funds and experienced workers to develop roads, transport, schools, medical services, and manufacturing. Finding competent government leaders was also very challenging.

Fighting disease and disaster

Diseases and natural disasters also affected many African nations. Many people suffered from malaria, **tuberculosis**, and AIDS. **Famines**, droughts, and floods also struck African countries.

Developed countries have organizations of scientists and doctors working to stop the spread of illnesses. Although African nations train doctors, they do not have the funds to develop such preventative measures. They must rely on developed nations and groups like the African Union for help during times of disaster.

Zimbabwean villagers carry home food rations from the international aid group Oxfam during a recent food shortage.

Apartheid in South Africa

Black South Africans suffered terribly under **apartheid**, a policy of separation that placed one race above another. By law non-whites, including Asians, Africans, and those of mixed race, had to live in separate, poorer areas, and use poorly funded schools, hospitals, transport, and libraries. Africans were placed at the bottom of this racial ranking.

The African National Congress (ANC) and other organizations led strikes and protests. Thousands were arrested and imprisoned, including the ANC leader, Nelson Mandela. Mandela and other ANC leaders were sentenced to life imprisonment in 1964.

Ending apartheid

Mandela's imprisonment inspired people around the world to join in the fight to end apartheid. Europeans banned the import of South African steel and gold. The United States passed laws banning loans to South Africa. People marched, demonstrated, and signed petitions.

After Mandela and the ANC leaders had been imprisoned for 26 years, President F. W. de Klerk finally recognised that apartheid had to end. To preserve his party's power, he freed Mandela in 1990. In 1994 Mandela was elected South Africa's first black president. Apartheid was over.

Nelson Mandela was elected president of South Africa in 1994.

Liberia

Americans founded the West African nation of Liberia in 1821 as a new home for freed slaves. Native peoples fought with the settlers, who **repressed** them and imposed their way of life on them.

An unequal society developed, with **Americo-Liberians** in control. Native Africans were barred from well-paying jobs and could not participate in government. Electricity and running water were set up only for the settlers. In 1979 violent demonstrations erupted and Samuel Doe seized power, killing President William Tolbert and his **cabinet**.

Doe killed anyone who challenged his authority. In 1989 another brutal leader, Charles Taylor, seized power after a seven-year civil war. After Taylor resigned due to international pressure in 2005, Ellen Johnson-Sirleaf was elected president.

Ellen Johnson-Sirleaf

Ellen Johnson-Sirleaf was an Americo-Liberian who went to work in the government of President William Tolbert in 1972. When Tolbert was murdered, she fled to Kenya. In 1984 she returned to campaign against Doe. She was imprisoned, then allowed to return to Kenya. After spending time working in the United States, she returned to run for president in 1997, but lost to Charles Taylor. In 2005 she ran again and won. She became the first woman elected president of an African nation.

Genocide in Rwanda

In countries such as Rwanda, ethnic tensions led to tragedy. The two main ethnic groups, the Hutus and the Tutsis, have been in conflict since Belgium took over the country from Germany in 1923.

The Tutsis were once a rich and powerful **minority**. When the Belgians took control, they expanded the power of the Tutsis, which angered the Hutus. In 1959 riots broke out, leaving 20,000 Tutsis dead. Many Tutsis fled to neighbouring countries and lived as **refugees**.

When Belgium granted Rwanda independence in 1962, the Tutsis lost their special status. Hutus became the new leaders. At the same time, the Tutsi refugees wanted to return home. They formed a group called the Rwandan **Patriotic** Front (RPF). Fighting between the two groups continued, with many thousands killed on each side.

These skulls are the remains of some of the hundreds of thousands killed in the Rwandan genocide of 1994.

In April 1994 the president's plane was shot down. Some said the Tutsis were responsible. This sparked the mass murder of Tutsis – men, women, and children – by the Hutus. Over 800,000 Tutsis died in the **genocide**. The RPF struck back, taking control of the country. Today, the nation is struggling to rebuild from this tragedy.

Kofi Annan

Kofi Annan is a leader dedicated to improving the lives of people around the world. Born in Ghana, Annan was educated in Africa, the United States, and Switzerland. In 1962 he started working for the **United Nations** (UN), an international organization that works to prevent wars, promote human rights, and fight hunger and disease. He worked to improve the health of people everywhere.

In 1996 Annan was appointed **Secretary General** of the UN. He worked to reform the organization. He reached out to new partners and spoke out for equality, human rights, and the rule of law.

Annan faced many world crises, from disease **epidemics** to wars. He organized an international response to violence in East Timor, an area on an island north of Australia. He called for businesses and governments around the world to respect environmental standards and human rights. He helped raise money and awareness of Africa's battle against AIDS. In 2001 Kofi Annan was awarded the Nobel Peace Prize for his work.

New approaches

The Civil Rights Movement helped African Americans gain many new rights. Racial **segregation** and **discrimination** were outlawed. But many African Americans were still frustrated by the racism and inequality that were still common around the United States.

On 3 April 1968, Martin Luther King considered the uncertain future, both for himself and for blacks. In his final speech, he said:

> I would like to live a long life ... But I'm not concerned about that now. I just want to do God's will. And he's allowed me to go up to the mountain. And I've looked over, and I've seen the promised land. I may not get there with you. But I want you to know tonight that we, as a people, will get to the promised land.

Martin Luther King assassinated

The next day, King was shot and killed while standing on a hotel balcony. As he had predicted, King would not live to reach the "promised land" of equal rights for all. Others would have to keep the dream alive.

Following Martin Luther King's death, riots and violence occurred in more than 100 US cities. Washington, D.C., home to a large African-American community, saw some of the worst rioting. President Lyndon Johnson sent thousands of troops to stop the violence. Many businesses were destroyed and jobs were lost. Both blacks and whites left the city for the suburbs.

Preserving King's legacy

Today, Martin Luther King represents African-American achievement, courage, leadership, and the ability of all Americans to overcome racial differences. The Martin Luther King, Jr, Center for Nonviolent Social Change, located in Atlanta, USA, was started in 1968 to keep the memory of King alive. It promotes his philosophy of using non-violence to promote social change.

The Black Panthers

Other African-American organizations working for equality believed that non-violence had failed, and a new approach was needed. Huey Newton and Bobby Seale, two African-American university students, formed the Black Panthers to fight police brutality. The members would wear blue shirts, black trousers, leather jackets, and berets, and carry loaded shotguns.

Active in the 1960s and 1970s, the Black Panthers demanded better treatment for blacks by carrying weapons, confronting police, and using force when necessary. They hoped to force government leaders to meet a list of demands to improve the lives of blacks and all people suffering from discrimination. They demanded free health care, education, jobs, decent housing, and an end to police brutality.

Many fights broke out between the Black Panthers and police. By 1970 more than 30 Black Panthers had died. Some broke away to work for government programmes to promote justice. By 1974 the party had fallen apart.

African-American men and women joined the Black Panthers to demand better treatment for blacks.

A new voice

As African Americans kept working for change, new leaders emerged. Rev Jesse Jackson, Sr, a minister who was close to King, worked to help inner city African Americans in Chicago lift themselves out of poverty. Jackson convinced many big Chicago companies to hire African Americans.

Jackson founded a new organization to improve lives for African Americans – Operation PUSH (People United to Serve Humanity). He soon became a leading voice for African Americans.

The Rainbow Coalition

In 1984 Jackson created the Rainbow **Coalition**. This group included Americans of many different races, skin colours, and religions. Native Americans, Asian Americans, Jewish Americans, and Arab Americans were among those invited to join African Americans in the fight for equal rights.

With the help of his coalition, Jackson ran for president in 1984 and in 1988. Each time he exceeded expectations. In 1988 he won the Democratic **primaries** in 11 out of the 50 states, proving that an African American could win broad support in a presidential race.

Jesse Jackson formed Operation PUSH and the Rainbow Coalition to improve the lives of African Americans.

Hundreds of thousands of African-American men took part in the Million Man March.

The Million Man March

In 1995 Louis Farrakhan, a **Nation of Islam** leader, gathered a huge crowd of African-American men together for the Million Man March in Washington, D.C., USA. Farrakhan organized the march to encourage African-American men to stay away from drugs and crime and to take care of their families. He hoped to promote black pride and unity among the men.

Fathers at home

In recent years, African Americans from Bill Cosby to Barack Obama have argued that too many African-American men are not staying with their families. In 2006 an estimated 65 per cent of African-American children were living in single parent homes.

Millions More

The Millions More Movement began in 2005 to mark the 10th anniversary of the Million Man March and bring awareness of the struggle of many African Americans to improve their lives. On 15 October 2005, an estimated one million men, women, and children gathered in Washington, D.C. They pledged to work to improve the lives of all African Americans.

Making up for the past

In recent years, many leaders have argued that the racism of the past is harming African Americans today. Because of past discrimination, they say, many blacks still have fewer opportunities than whites. In addition, African-American families were never paid for generations of slave labour.

Affirmative action

In the United States and elsewhere, **affirmative action** programmes were developed to make sure that people of all backgrounds have a chance to succeed. Schools and businesses are given incentives or required to offer some positions to qualified **minority** candidates. Some complain that people should be judged based on qualifications alone, not race. Others argue that the programmes make up for social inequalities and prevent racist hiring practices. In 2008 several states voted to eliminate affirmative action laws.

African-American innovation

Despite discrimination and lack of resources, many African Americans have contributed to society by developing important inventions. Here are a few notable African-American inventors:

- Jan Ernst Matzeliger (1852–99) invented a shoemaking machine.

- George Washington Carver (1864–1943) born a slave, invented peanut butter.

- Madame C. J. Walker (1867–1919) invented a hair-growing lotion and became the first female African-American millionaire.

- Garrett Morgan (1877–1963) invented the gas mask.

- Emmett Chappelle (b. 1925) invented new ways to detect bacteria in foods and in the human body.

- Dr. Patricia E. Bath (b. 1949) invented a form of eye surgery that allows many blind people to see.

Reparations

Some leaders have also sought to win approval for **reparations** (payments) to African Americans for the harm slavery caused. On 30 July 2008, the US House of Representatives issued an apology for American slavery and laws that supported racial discrimination, but did not address reparations.

Colin Powell and Condoleezza Rice

Colin Powell was the first African American to serve as Secretary of State, one of the most powerful advisors to the president of the United States. He was followed by Condoleezza Rice, the first African-American woman to serve in the position. Both Powell and Rice worked for President George W. Bush.

Colin Powell was born in Harlem, New York, in 1937 to a family of Jamaican immigrants. After university Powell joined the army, rising through the ranks over a 35-year career. Finally, he was named Chairman of the Joint Chiefs of Staff, the highest position in the United States military. He believed that the United States should only send soldiers to war for specific reasons and then apply overwhelming force to win quick victories. This idea became known as the Powell Doctrine. In 2000 he accepted the position of Bush's first Secretary of State.

Condoleezza Rice was born in 1954 in Alabama, in the southern United States, when racial discrimination was at its worst. She thrived in many areas, becoming an expert in Russian history and politics as well as an accomplished pianist. In 2000 she was named President Bush's National Security Advisor, and in 2005, she was appointed Secretary of State after Powell resigned. She worked to resolve ongoing international issues, from the Israeli-Palestinian conflict to North Korea's nuclear programme.

Racism in Britain

In the 1970s, the British government further restricted immigration, but immigrants continued to arrive. Many came from India and Pakistan, while others came from the Caribbean. Africans from nations such as Angola and Somalia fled their homelands to escape violent civil wars and military takeovers. Between 1991 and 2001, immigration made up more than half of the country's population growth.

Thanks to the Race Relations Act, it was illegal to refuse housing, employment, or public services to anyone because of race. But new immigrants from around the world often felt unwelcome in Great Britain. Some whites have called for further restrictions on immigration.

Blacks in poverty

Today, many black Britons are in poverty. According to a 2007 report, 45 per cent of Britons from Africa and 30 per cent of those from the Caribbean live in poverty. Only 40 per cent of African Britons worked full-time. Even those workers with degrees earned less than whites with the same degrees.

Protestors march against the immigration of non-whites to Britain, in London in 1972.

British police work to end the rioting in Brixton, London.

"Racist policing"

British law gives police the right to stop and search people they suspect of having committed a crime. Some Black Britons feel that police unfairly stop and search them. They call this "racist policing". In recent years, this belief has led to rioting.

The Brixton area of London has a high crime rate. It is also home to many poor, unemployed people. To reduce crime, large numbers of police walked the streets and stopped people they suspected of a crime. Some black Britons felt that police stopped and searched them because of their race. Angered by what they felt was racism, residents of Brixton rioted in 1981, 1985, and 1995.

The death of Stephen Lawrence

In 1993 a black teenager named Stephen Lawrence was stabbed to death at a bus stop near his home in London. Police arrested, then released, five white youths suspected of killing him. Even though a judge ruled that Lawrence was "unlawfully killed in a completely unprovoked racist attack by five white youths", the suspects never went to jail. Stephen's parents led a campaign to prevent racist police practices, and police policies slowly changed. An independent inquiry found the Metropolitan Police Force guilty of "institutional racism".

Campaigns to end racism

Although racial **discrimination** still exists in Great Britain, many groups are working to end it. Using popular pastimes such as sports and music, groups can spread an anti-discrimination message to a large number of people.

Let's Kick Racism Out of Football is a campaign started by British football teams. Kick It Out works to bring these clubs and communities together to end discrimination. They make sure that young people of all races have the chance to play football.

People can report acts of racism to Kick It Out, whether among players or spectators. The organization campaigns to ensure that no tolerance is shown to racists. Kick It Out is also a member of the Football Against Racism in Europe group.

Love Music Hate Racism is another campaign against discrimination. It was started by the **Anti-Nazi League**. They believe that the energy of modern music can help bring people of different races together. Over 150 concerts have been held since 2002.

Love Music Hate Racism concerts are attended by people of all races.

Black British Members of Parliament

Several Black Britons have served as Members of Parliament (MPs). Bernie Grant and Diane Abbott were two of the first Black British MPs.

Grant moved to Britain in 1963 from Guyana in South America. He studied engineering, but left university in protest over racial discrimination against black students. Grant became a union leader and fought for the rights of his fellow workers. In 1983 he was elected to Parliament. He spoke out against policing tactics he said were racist. He also called for more help for people in the inner cities.

Diane Abbott became the first black British woman MP in 1987. Her family moved to Britain from Jamaica in the early 1950s. Abbott is famous for speaking out against British immigration laws. In her first speech in Parliament, Abbott argued that Britain's immigration policies were racist. She also worked to investigate gun-related crimes and improve education for black British children.

Bernie Grant

Developing the Caribbean

While many Caribbean people moved to Europe in search of better lives, those who remained behind faced great challenges. After years of **colonial** rule, these small nations still largely depended on their agriculture to survive. In recent decades, an increase in tourism has boosted some economies. Some nations have also tried to speed development by creating shared universities, banks, and other institutions.

Jamaica

Jamaica, a nation of fertile farmland and white sandy beaches, is one of the Caribbean nations still struggling to prosper. Jamaica has large sugar and coffee plantations. Because the foreigners who export these crops own the plantations, Jamaicans themselves see little financial benefit. Many live in rural villages with no electricity and grow their own food to survive.

As the population grows there is less land for families to farm. Many Jamaicans (and other islanders) have moved away, as they have done since slavery ended in 1838. They send money home to help their families still in Jamaica. Today more than one million Jamaicans live in Britain, the United States, and Canada.

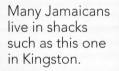

Many Jamaicans live in shacks such as this one in Kingston.

Most Haitians work small plots of land to grow food for their families.

Political instability in Haiti

Haiti is an island of nearly nine million people. Boys farm, and girls sell crops and handmade crafts. Most are peasants and many children do not go to school. Because the forests are cut for firewood and farmland, soil washes down the mountains when it rains, making it harder for the peasant farmers to grow enough food to feed their families.

In recent years, Haiti has suffered under the rule of **dictators**. François "Papa Doc" Duvalier took power in 1957 and declared himself president for life. Many educated people fled Haiti, leaving few skilled professionals behind. In 1971 he was replaced by his son, Jean-Claude "Baby Doc" Duvalier. In 1986 mass uprisings forced Jean-Claude to flee from Haiti.

In 1990 Haiti held its first free election. Catholic priest Jean-Bertrand Aristide became president. Many believed Aristide was a friend of the poor, but he was removed from power in a **coup d'état** and fled the country. In 1994, under international pressure, he was allowed to return to power. He was elected again in 2000, but he was forced out in 2004. Today Aristide lives in Africa, but many Haitians hope he will return one day.

Meeting social challenges

By the late 1960s, millions of blacks lived in poor inner city neighbourhoods. Some were able to find skilled jobs and move away. But by 1990, four times as many inner city African Americans lived in poverty as their neighbours in the suburbs. Similarly in Britain, many areas of London and Birmingham are populated mainly by black Britons and other non-white **minorities**. These areas provided fewer job opportunities, leaving many residents in poverty.

Many businesses left the inner city for other areas or even other countries, leaving fewer jobs for blacks. Some families were forced to rely on benefits to make ends meet. As poverty spread, so did racial prejudice. Inner city slums became more isolated from the rest of society.

Inner cities are often home to many poor non-white minorities.

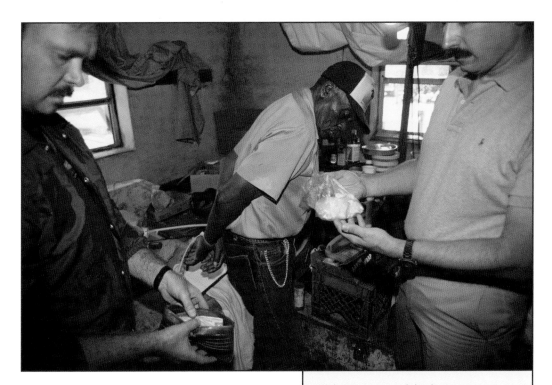

Police arrest a black man following the seizure of illegal drugs.

The war on drugs

Alongside unemployment and poverty, drug abuse is another major problem in inner cities. Since the 1970s, Western governments have waged a war to control the flow of illegal drugs into their countries. Leaders believe there is a strong connection between drug addiction, criminal activity, and poverty. As police departments spend more time and money fighting drugs, the number of people in prison is rising.

One out of every 100 Americans is in prison, and half of these prisoners are there on drug charges. In contrast, 12 per cent of black men between the ages of 20 and 34 are in prison. While most Americans addicted to drugs are employed whites, most of the prisoners serving time for drug charges are black.

Even though the prison population continues to grow, so does drug use. Many leaders question whether the war on drugs has worked.

Black Britons in prison

Since 1993 the number of people in prison in Great Britain has more than doubled. One out of every ten British prisoners is black. Over half were convicted of drug-related crimes.

School busing

By law schools in the United States must be open to all children, regardless of race. But many white

In many US cities, black and white students were bused to other neighbourhoods to promote school integration.

leaders in the southern states refused to obey this law. They made plans to integrate schools, but many were slow to take action.

In 1969 the Supreme Court updated this law. Their decision in *Alexander v. Holmes County Board of Education* stated that schools must be integrated immediately. So schools in the South began to accept black and white students in the same classrooms.

However, in many places, black children and white children lived in different neighbourhoods. So if children went to schools in their own neighbourhoods, most classrooms would still be all black or all white. To solve this problem school busing programmes started.

During the 1970s and 1980s, children were bused from one neighbourhood to another to make sure that school classrooms included both black and white children.

The Rodney King case

On 3 March 1991 in Los Angeles, USA, a confrontation between an African-American man and white police officers sparked controversy and violence. The police stopped Rodney King after a high-speed chase. When police tried to handcuff King, he resisted. Police said he came after the officers, forcing them to beat him repeatedly.

George Holliday videotaped the incident from his nearby flat. His tape shows four police officers grabbing and beating King while others stood nearby and watched. The tape was broadcast around the country, outraging the African-American community.

Rioting erupts

The four police officers were charged with excessive use of force. But none were convicted. This triggered massive rioting in Los Angeles. Fifty-three people died, and fire and looting destroyed hundreds of businesses.

The Los Angeles riots showed that poverty and unrest in the United States' inner cities was still a major problem.

Rioters destroyed millions of dollars worth of property in the Los Angeles riots.

Seizing opportunities

Following the Civil Rights Movement, opportunities for African Americans expanded. While many lived in poor areas, others escaped lives of poverty through education, hard work, and sometimes the support of programmes such as **affirmative action**.

In 1980 just half of all African Americans were finishing secondary school, and 8 out of every 100 African-American adults had graduated from university. In 2006 8 out of 10 African Americans were finishing secondary school and 19 out of every 100 had graduated from university.

"Buppies"

Around the world, more black people are earning degrees, working in professional jobs, and joining the middle class. Many live in wealthier urban areas. These people are sometimes referred to as Black Urban Professionals, or "Buppies".

Today, many blacks around the world are doctors, lawyers, government officials, and business executives.

Does racism persist?

Despite the improvements in the lives of some black men and women around the world, many still feel that they are treated as second-class citizens. In the United States, for example, some African Americans feel that the voting system is still unfair. Some feel their votes have been unfairly discounted in elections. Others say they have been denied the opportunity to vote at all.

Similarly, when disaster strikes, some African Americans feel they are not treated fairly by their own government. This charge was raised in 2005 when Hurricane Katrina lashed the US coastline. This natural disaster devastated poor African-American communities in Louisiana and Mississippi in the southern United States. The government was slow to respond.

In 2005 Hurricane Katrina devastated African-American communities in New Orleans, USA.

Hurricane Katrina

When the powerful Hurricane Katrina struck New Orleans, Louisiana, **levees** meant to prevent flooding broke down. Many homes and neighbourhoods were destroyed, especially in African-American areas.

Thousands of people were trapped by the flooding, and many died. In the areas unreachable by rescuers, bodies were left in the water for days. In some areas unaffected by flooding, witnesses said, suspicious whites blocked off roads and shot at African Americans seeking refuge. It took days before officials restored order and rescued many suffering victims. By then more than 1,500 people had died.

Some African Americans pointed to the government's response as a sign of racism. They believed that if more of the victims were wealthy or white, a speedy rescue mission would have saved many more lives.

Artists and scholars

While many black people worked their way into the professional middle class, some others have achieved great fame and wealth. Two of the most successful are Oprah Winfrey and Will Smith.

Oprah Winfrey

Oprah Winfrey, the world's first African-American billionaire, grew up poor in a small Mississippi town. She worked her way up from local radio and television jobs to become the host of the country's most popular talk show. She also started Oprah's Book Club, which inspires millions of Americans to read. Her Angel Network raises millions of dollars to help young people. Some of this money is used for education scholarships and some is used to support schools and **AIDS** programmes for South African children.

Millions of viewers of all races tune in to *The Oprah Winfrey Show*.

Will Smith

Will Smith was born in Philadelphia, USA, and found success as a teenage rapper and television actor. He later moved into film work, as an actor and later a producer. Smith was one of the first African-American leading men in Hollywood. He has had a string of box-office successes around the world. He has twice been nominated for an Oscar, including a nomination for his portrayal of Muhammad Ali, the famous African-American boxer, in the film *Ali*.

New music emerges

Black musicians continued to experiment with new musical forms. Two popular musical styles to emerge were reggae and hip hop.

Reggae

Reggae music developed in Jamaica in the 1960s. This slow, bouncy style grew out of faster ska music, and draws on traditional African and Caribbean music. Bob Marley, perhaps the best-known reggae artist, wrote songs about love, political upheaval, and freedom – both physical and spiritual. "**Emancipate** yourself from mental slavery. None but ourselves can free our minds," Marley sang, quoting Jamaican leader Marcus Garvey. Marley believed that blacks could achieve a kind of freedom by looking within.

Bob Marley remains one of the best-known reggae artists decades after his death from cancer in 1981.

Rap music

Rap music was born in New York City, USA. Disc jockeys playing records at parties began playing the percussion (drumming) parts of a song and speaking along with the beat. They mixed the music using record turntables. Soon, a free-flowing style of spoken word and rhythms emerged. A cultural style known as hip hop grew up around rap with its own language, fashion, and mindset. Rap artists and groups such as Run DMC, Public Enemy, and Dr. Dre became known all over the world.

Black writers

In 1965 African-American writer LeRoi Jones moved to Harlem, New York, to form a new literary movement. The "Black Arts" movement was an expression of a powerful black identity. Rather than blending in with literature dominated by white writers, Black Arts writers explored the heritage of blacks everywhere. This movement inspired a generation of new writers, including Toni Morrison, Alice Walker, and Maya Angelou.

Toni Morrison

Toni Morrison grew up in a close-knit black community in Ohio, USA. She learned the importance of storytelling from her father, who told her folktales of the African-American community. Morrison's complex stories about Americans seeking love and justice in the world won her the Nobel Prize for Literature in 1993.

Benjamin Zephaniah

Benjamin Zephaniah was born and raised in Birmingham, England. As a teenager he was already performing reggae-influenced poetry, and during the 1980s he became a well-known figure in the media. His poetry was political and commented on the events of the time. More recently Zephaniah has become a celebrated children's poet and novelist, and he is a vocal campaigner for animal rights.

Over 22 days in 1991 Benjamin Zephaniah performed on every continent.

Black Studies programmes

In the late 1960s, some African-American students and teachers complained that too many university courses were taught from a white perspective. No classes focused on black literature, history, and culture. Some universities listened and began to offer a new kind of class. The first Black Studies classes began at San Francisco State University in 1969.

These programmes grew to cover topics concerning all people with African heritage, not just African Americans. Today Black Studies programmes include Afro-American Research, African-American Studies, Africana Studies, Afro-American Studies, and Black Studies. Some include classes in Latin American and Caribbean cultures and are called **Ethnic** Studies.

Cornel West

As a secondary school student in Sacramento, USA, Cornel West and several friends went on strike to protest the lack of Black Studies classes. He went on to direct the Black Studies programmes at top US universities Princeton and Harvard. West has also written many books and articles about race in the United States.

Africa today

Between 1975 and 2005, the population of Africa more than doubled, from about 416 million to 922 million people. Most of these people are poor. The average African earns less than £340 each year, and hunger is widespread.

War zones

As recently as 2008, 14 nations, including Chad, Sudan, and the Congo, were involved in civil wars or wars with neighbouring countries. Almost a quarter of all Africans live in war zones. In some countries, bands of soldiers often loot and kill villagers. The soldiers also kidnap children, distribute guns, and force children to join in the fighting.

In countries such as Uganda and Sierra Leone, children have been forced to fight in wars.

Dictatorships

Local people suffer greatly under the rule of **dictators** in some African nations. These dictators limit freedoms, slow development, and have ruined entire economies.

Free elections?

In some countries, leaders have been accused of using unfair tactics to win elections. In Zimbabwe, for example, a 2008 election kept President Robert Mugabe in power. However, the opposing party withdrew from the race after they said they were violently attacked. In Kenya, Mwai Kbaki was declared the winner of a 2007 presidential election. But allegations that the vote was rigged led to rioting throughout Kenya.

Fighting for resources

Africa is a land rich in natural resources such as diamonds, gold, oil, and minerals. But most native Africans have seen little benefit from these resources. Part of the problem is that foreign **corporations** still control most of the resources. Corrupt leadership has sometimes concentrated much of the remaining wealth in the hands of a few Africans.

Blood diamonds

Sierra Leone is rich in diamond mines. In 1991 rebel soldiers with support from Liberia gained control of the mines. Their attacks sparked a civil war. The rebels forced local people to mine the diamonds under brutal conditions and sold the diamonds to support their war efforts. In Angola conflict over diamond mines led to a civil war. In 2001 the **United Nations** set up rules to ensure that diamond sales do not fund civil wars.

Oil conflicts

Some African nations, such as Nigeria, Sudan, and the Democratic Republic of Congo, are rich in oil. In Nigeria control of oil resources is in the hands of a few wealthy people with connections to the government and international oil companies. In Sudan a civil war between Arabs living in the North and black farmers in the South worsened when oil was discovered in the South.

Workers spend long hours panning for diamonds at a mine in the Ivory Coast.

AIDS

Perhaps the most serious crisis afflicting Africa is the **AIDS epidemic**. Each year more than a million Africans die of this deadly disease.

AIDS and the virus that causes it, HIV, first appeared in Africa in the late 1970s. This disease prevents a person's body from fighting off germs and infections. It is passed from one person to another through blood and sexual contact.

This disease spread rapidly because many Africans did not understand how it is passed on. In countries such as South Africa, Zambia, and Zimbabwe, as many as 20 per cent of adults are infected with the virus. In recent years, international groups have led efforts to educate people on how to prevent the disease.

The drugs used to treat AIDS are expensive. Because of the poverty in Africa, people must hope for other nations to provide these drugs or hope for drug companies to provide them cheaply.

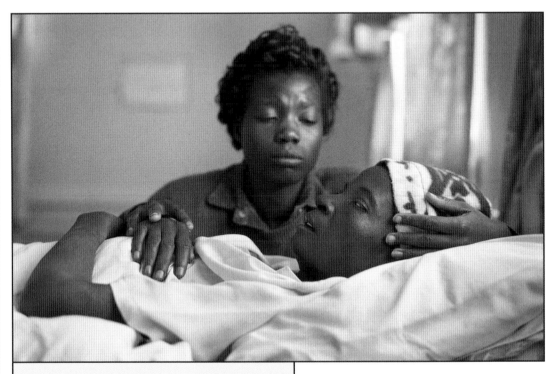

A woman with AIDS is comforted by her sister in a hospital in Zimbabwe.

Malaria

Malaria is another disease common in Africa. It is caused by a bite from a mosquito infected with a parasite. Most deaths from malaria are in African children under five years old.

Nelson Mandela's Children's Fund

In 1995 Nelson Mandela created the Nelson Mandela Children's Fund (NMCF) to help improve the lives of children in South Africa. NMCF works to help children orphaned by AIDS. It sends them to school, gives them a place to live, and provides food to eat.

Every year Mandela and his wife Graca throw a huge Christmas party for South Africa's poor children. In 2004 nearly 20,000 children, many of them AIDS orphans, attended this party at Mandela's farm in Qunu, South Africa.

Mandela welcomed each child to the party with gifts of food, books, and clothing. The children watched a puppet show by Kami, the first Sesame Street Muppet with AIDS. They also listened to the singing of a nine-year-old whose parents had died of AIDS.

The party drew worldwide attention to the work of the NMCF. The NMCF has groups worldwide. Members in Great Britain, the United States, Australia, and Canada work to raise money to help South Africa's children.

Nelson Mandela dances to a children's choir during the NMCF's Christmas party.

Building the future

Building a better future for Africans will be challenging. Over 300 million Africans live on less than one dollar (68 pence) each day. War, disease, corruption, and foreign influence have all been obstacles to development.

Developed nations can assist Africa in many ways. They can forgive the debt that many poor African nations are struggling to repay. They can supply aid to help fight the spread of **AIDS** and feed victims of **famine**. They can also remove trade barriers to allow Africans to export food, minerals, and other resources around the world.

Nigerian writers

Nigerian writers Chinua Achebe and Wole Soyinka have made a difference through their art. Achebe's novels focus on his native people, the Ibo, and the effect of Western influences. *Things Fall Apart* (1958) is considered one of the most important African novels.

Wole Soyinka has written more than 20 plays. Many are based on the mythology of his native tribe, the Yoruba. He also has worked for peace in Nigeria, trying to help opposing sides avoid civil war in 1967. He spent 22 months in prison for his efforts. Soyinka won the Nobel Prize for Literature in 1986.

Chinua Achebe

Ghana looks forward

The West African nation of Ghana is one example of the potential of African nations. Once an outpost in the slave trade, in 1957 Ghana became the first African nation to achieve independence from Great Britain. In the late 1960s and the 1970s, Ghana suffered corruption and instability, as one leader after another took control by force.

In the 1980s, the country began to show signs of stability. In 1992 a new **constitution** was approved. Ghana became a **democracy**, and a free press flourished. When civil wars broke out in neighbouring countries, Ghana sent troops to help maintain peace. Today Ghana exports cocoa, gold, timber, and other resources around the world. In 2007 oil was discovered off Ghana's coast, which many hope will further boost the economy.

Challenges ahead

Although Ghana's economy is stronger than other nations in the region, a third of the people still live on less than a dollar (68 pence) a day. Many of its most educated workers have moved to Western countries, resulting in a "brain drain".

"We have moved along the track a little way," President John Kufuor said in 2007. "But we have a long way to go."

Ghana is a nation that includes both poor rural areas and cities with bustling marketplaces.

Barack Obama delivers the main speech at the 2004 Democratic National Convention.

Hope for African Americans

The future for African Americans is a hopeful one. Many racist practices have largely become a thing of the past. More blacks and whites live and work side by side. African-American literature, art, and music are flourishing. However, more African Americans are still poor, unemployed, or in prison than other **ethnic** groups. Fewer African Americans have health care or good jobs. True equality for all Americans is still a dream.

Barack Obama

In 2004 a new African-American voice emerged. At a speech at the Democratic National Convention, Barack Obama, a newly elected politician, spoke of a nation that was no longer divided by race. "There's not a black America and a white America ... There's the United States of America," he said. Obama was the son of a white American woman and a black Kenyan man. Many people hoped that a leader with this unique background could help bring all races together.

Obama's experience

Barack Obama was a highly educated man who had also seen life in the inner city. He graduated from Harvard University and became a civil rights lawyer. Later he worked as a community organizer in poor neighbourhoods in Chicago, Illinois. He was elected to the United States **Senate** after serving in the Illinois State Senate for eight years. Then he decided to run for president in the 2008 election.

The 2008 campaign

Obama ran for President with a hopeful message of change. He called for better health care and education. He wanted politicians to stop arguing and start working together again. His motto, "Yes We Can", made his supporters believe that anything was possible.

On 4 November 2008, Obama proved his supporters right. Forty-five years after African Americans could not vote freely, people of all races voted for the first African-American President. On the night of his victory, Obama said, "If there is anyone out there who still doubts that America is a place where all things are possible ... tonight is your answer." His election may not have ended the struggle for racial equality, but it proved that for blacks everywhere, the future held great promise.

Barack Obama and his wife, Michelle, greet crowds during his inauguration.

Black Britons

Blacks in Great Britain face many challenges as they look to the future. Like African Americans, many black Britons live in poor inner city areas. Others are part of the middle class, with skilled jobs and good homes. But many still face racial **discrimination**.

The Equality and Human Rights Commission is working to end this discrimination and build a better future. It works to make sure that laws banning racial discrimination and protecting human rights are enforced.

"Equally Different" is one of the commission's campaigns to encourage equality, fairness, and human rights for all. It presents a collection of stories from people of all races and social backgrounds. By watching these stories online, people learn what it is like to be of a different race or social background.

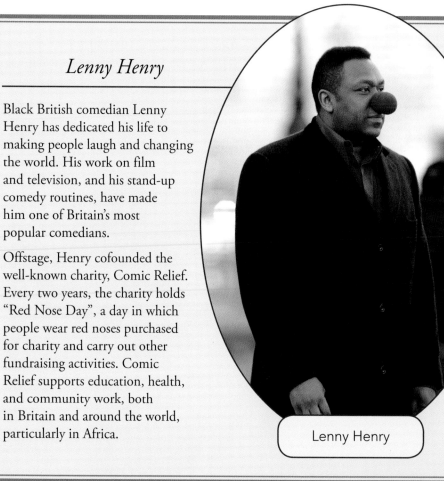

Lenny Henry

Black British comedian Lenny Henry has dedicated his life to making people laugh and changing the world. His work on film and television, and his stand-up comedy routines, have made him one of Britain's most popular comedians.

Offstage, Henry cofounded the well-known charity, Comic Relief. Every two years, the charity holds "Red Nose Day", a day in which people wear red noses purchased for charity and carry out other fundraising activities. Comic Relief supports education, health, and community work, both in Britain and around the world, particularly in Africa.

Lenny Henry

Blacks around the world

The future for blacks around the world holds a mix of despair and hope. Millions of Africans suffer from AIDS and live in crippling poverty. Blacks in the Caribbean and Brazil often earn barely enough to feed their families. Even in developed nations, many blacks live in poor inner city neighbourhoods.

But millions more blacks around the world have moved on to better lives. They have gone to school and found work as teachers, police officers, scientists, doctors, lawyers, and many other careers. Some, such as Barack Obama, have reached the highest levels of government. Many African leaders are building more prosperous nations.

Millions look to these examples and remain hopeful that building a better future for blacks around the world is possible. Progress towards this goal will be achieved if people of all races work together to help those in need.

Today's black youth, like these children in Botswana, will face a brighter future if people around the world can work together.

Timeline

1968	Martin Luther King is assassinated.
1969	*Alexander v. Holmes County Board of Education* Supreme Court decision calls for school desegregation.
1969	The first African American Studies classes begin at San Francisco State University in California, USA.
1971	Jean-Claude "Papa Doc" Duvalier becomes the President of Haiti.
1973	The Bahamas becomes an independent member of the **British Commonwealth**.
1974	Judge Arthur Garrity rules that Boston public schools practise racial **discrimination** and orders forced busing of students.
1974	The African nation Guinea Bissau wins its independence from Portugal.
1975	The African nations São Tomé, Príncipe, Cape Verde, Angola, and Mozambique win their independence from Portugal, Comores from France, and Western Sahara from Spain.
1976	The African nation Seychelles wins its independence from Britain.
1977	The African nation Djibouti wins its independence from France.
1978	Louis Farrakhan becomes the leader of the **Nation of Islam**.
1979	St. Lucia and St. Vincent and the Grenadines achieve independence from Britain.
1980	The African nation Zimbabwe wins its independence from Britain.
1981	Riots take place in Brixton, London.
1981	Belize becomes an independent member of the British Commonwealth.
1982	St. Christopher and Nevis become a fully independent state and member of the British Commonwealth.
1984	Jesse Jackson runs for President of the United States.
1986	Wole Soyinka wins the Nobel Prize in Literature.
1988	Jesse Jackson runs for President of the United States for the second time.
1990	President F. W. de Klerk of South Africa frees Nelson Mandela from prison.

1990	Namibia wins its independence from South Africa.
1991	Rebel soldiers from Liberia invade Sierra Leone and take control of the diamond mines.
1992	Caribbean poet Derek Walcott wins the Nobel Prize in Literature.
1992	Riots break out after Los Angeles police beat Rodney King.
1993	The African nation Eritrea wins its independence from Ethiopia.
1993	Black writer Toni Morrison wins the Nobel Prize in Literature.
1994	Over 800,000 die in Rwandan **genocide**.
1994	**Apartheid** ends in South Africa.
1994	The population of Africa grows to over 700 million.
1995	Louis Farrakhan leads the Million Man March in Washington, D.C., USA
1997	Kofi Annan becomes **Secretary General** of the **United Nations**.
2001	The United Nations bans the sale of Liberian blood diamonds.
2002	The Organization of African Unity (OAU) is renamed the African Union (AU).
2004	Barack Obama is elected to the United States **Senate**.
2004	Oprah Winfrey becomes the world's first black billionaire.
2005	Hurricane Katrina strikes the southern United States, causing flooding in New Orleans that destroys African-American neighbourhoods.
2005	Ellen Johnson-Sirleaf becomes Africa's and Liberia's first female president.
2008	Barack Obama is elected President of the United States.

Glossary

affirmative action laws that require racial diversity in hiring employees

AIDS serious disease of the immune system caused by the HIV virus

Americo-Liberian someone with American and Liberian heritage

Anti-Nazi League organization set up to fight prejudice, particularly the idea that whites are the supreme race

apartheid system in which different ethnic groups are kept separate

British Commonwealth group of former British colonies that pay allegiance to the British Crown

cabinet group of senior government ministers

coalition group of people or nations joining together as one

colonial relating to an outside ruler

constitution ideas according to which a country or state is governed

corporation large business

coup d'état forceful takeover of a government

democracy form of government in which citizens hold the power

dictator person who rules by force and violence

discrimination act of treating some people better than others for no good reason

emancipate make someone or something free

epidemic serious outbreak of disease

ethnic member of a group of people who have shared customs, language, and traditions

famine serious shortage of food causing severe hunger and death

genocide planned extermination of an entire racial or ethnic group

levee barrier used to prevent flooding by oceans and rivers

malaria disease spread by mosquitoes that causes chills, fever, and sweating

minority group that makes up less than half a population

Nation of Islam religious group formed in the United States, consisting of black members

patriotic feeling, expressing, or inspired by love of one's country

primary vote to determine who will represent a political party in a United States presidential election

refugee person who has fled to a new country to be safe

reparation payment proposed for African Americans in repayment for slavery

repress prevent someone's freedom and prosperity

Secretary General leader of an organization such as the United Nations

segregation separation of races

senate part of the United States governing body, similar to the House of Lords

tuberculosis disease caused by bacteria that damages the lungs

United Nations group of nations dedicated to achieving global peace, freedom, and prosperity

Find out more

Books

Africa Focus: Modern Africa, Rob Bowden and Rosie Wilson (Heinemann Library, 2010)

Barack Obama, Stephen Feinstein (Enslow, 2008)

Great Lives: Nelson Mandela, Ann Kramer (QED Publishing, 2005)

Websites

BBC Black history homepage
http://www.bbc.co.uk/1xtra/blackhistory/index.shtml

Stories from a range of people
http://www.equalityhumanrights.com/en/projects/equallydifferent/Pages/
EquallyDifferentarchive.aspx

Index